Excursions by ToPoJo ——
An imprint series from Tokyo Poetry Journal
https://www.topojo.com/excursions

ISBN 978−1−957704−00−5

Designed by Xiao Yue Shan
Edited by Jordan A. Y. Smith
Copyedited by Joy Waller

Website www.topojo.com
Facebook @tokyopoetryjournal
Twitter @poetrytokyo
Instagram @tokyopoetry

ROOMS
WITH
NO
NEIGHBORS

WITH
NO
NEIGHBORS

ROOMS
WITH
NO

CONTENTS

Water take-off	10
The path to Tivoli Park	11
Shallow sleep	12
Standing on the surface of the lake	14
The path to Tivoli Park 2	18
A quality cuisine	20
Sabbath	22
The time of bones	23
At port	24
Train #2214	26
Jumbled forest	28
To the island of graves	30
Hotel Elite	31
I am culpable	34
Thick fog	35
Spring storm	36

Straße des 17. Juni 37

To the north 38

Ibis Hotel 40

Train #2348 42

Sundial 43

Blackbirds 45

South of the Spree River 46

Alexanderplatz Station 47

Anywhere to be found 48

The room of 18 April 49

Moving away from the linden tree 50

Water landing 52

Afterword 55

Data 56

Translator's Note 57

To the neighbors I have yet to meet

and to the neighbors I will not meet.

Water take-off

carried by clouds that heap
fine fabric
stained by the sunset
when one desire is realized
that is one step closer to despair

the raising of the curtain
is always blurry
and yet the unmoving waves of clouds
everyone, altogether,
settles into nondescript chairs
already heading toward the end
as if nothing like summer existed
a powdery snow falls softly
at the end of march
a powdery snow falls softly
through eternity
accepting the softly falling snow
the runway lights await

The path to Tivoli Park

clinging to a tall, tall tree
a bird of shadow and the dazzling of white

it's better not to concern yourself with time
he said
and then, after that, he said farewell
we had just met
at 7:41 this morning
the bells pealed
the town was wrapped
utterly unmoving
clicking his tongue
with a smiling face
he hands out fresh-baked bread
it's better not to concern yourself with time
he says once more
the fresh-baked bread
still fresh-baked

a bell rings out gently
there is no clock in sight

Shallow sleep

because birds swell up when it is cold
the birds of this town are round, round
their yellow beaks distend
against a color darker than night
they walk in front of the post office
there are, after all, birds that don't fly

not knowing is foolish, childish,
beautiful
still fearful of knowing
in an unknown town
we swell up when it is cold and so
i also distend and, on waking,
become round, round

the snow continues to fall for days
but i don't know

NAPRODAJ

Standing on the surface of the lake

i awoke crying
having forgotten my dream
clearly you had said something awful
it seems to me

on the frozen surface of the lake
the veins of leaves
living upside down
in an overcast sky
are as they should be
please stop the car
cameras in hand
we stand side-by-side
and open our eyes
my nose is red
a swelling heat behind the eyes
only the urge
to cry remains

people the world over
like this, camera in hand,
will stop the car and stare
we, who did just that,
will forget the next day

clearly you had said something awful
a swelling heat behind the eyes
i adjust my knit cap
down more deeply
there is a spot of sun
invited by the mirage
of water on the road
please stop the car
because now i'm
going to wail

The path to Tivoli Park 2

on the first sunlit day
i set out in search of water and sugar
and ended up losing my way
finding and seeking out even more light
the smell of a zoo

suppressing my hunger
i press on still lost
at the opening of a back, back alley
an old woman on a bicycle
speaks to me in a language
i can't understand
giving me directions
or talking about the weather
in a terribly hoarse voice
a person who might be someone
perhaps not there
she kisses me
and leaves
i am lost

incapable of both
dying and living
the days flow single-mindedly on
still lost
i stand in the midst of the warm light
when i finally arrive home
bearing weighty water and sugar
a thousand years have passed

incapable of both
dying and living
the days flow single-mindedly on
when i open a certain familiar door
with a hoarse voice you say
welcome back

a person who might be someone
perhaps not there

A quality cuisine

as much as possible
don't talk about the weather
because it leads so easily
to other things

"for the next three days
the rain will continue
and then turn to snow"

each morning
concerned about
the patterns of the sky
like trying to read
someone else's face
as much as possible
don't talk about the weather

we go to meet
the beloved beasts
who protect us
making sounds with
their entire bodies

they carry spring to us
for the sake of
a quality cuisine

in the end, walking the same road
the hands of the clock
obsessively marking
there is never enough time
the rain beating loudly
a broken green umbrella
my breath is white
despite my hatred of gloves
i end up buying gloves
warm, alpaca ones that
cover as completely as possible
i hold hands with you
my cold fingertips
unnoticed

at the quality table
we unwittingly end up
talking about the weather
reading even the face
of the season
"the beloved beasts
will call forth the spring
so rest assured"

concerned about the time
we eat our meal
as we should
we don't want to talk
about the weather
about the seasons
as much as possible
our breath is white
we hold hands

Sabbath

i return from the tedious tower
and my body, my body is chilled
still unable to accept
i carefully put away eggs
dyed with onion
two days ago
i carefully put away eggs
dyed with cabbage
when should i eat them?
everyone silent with baskets in hand
gathering, one then the next
there is wordless understanding
but there would be more understanding
with words
like a couple
who have lived together
for a long time
there is wordless understanding
but there would be more understanding
with words
the husbands i have yet to meet
are scattered around the world
conversation diminishes
the sound of rain and tail lights
turning left, a church

The time of bones

over the course of
the middle of the night
sixty minutes disappeared
when autumn comes again
it seems those sixty minutes
will return

on a tranquil sunday
we sway with the movement of the bus
heavy clouds that seem ready
to come crashing down
hang above us

because of deteriorated bones,
i must awaken on sunday
pry open heavy eyelids
and take medications
the time given over to
stationary bones
when i die
from my burnt body
lustrous bones
will be discovered
more than thirty thousand years ago
bones were used as flutes
will my bones also sing?

thinking about thirty thousand years
caught up in sixty disappeared minutes
we sway with the movement of the train

losing sixty minutes while remaining stationary
this wonderful, bothersome sunday

At port

this isn't my room
while i can glimpse the square
from my window
i'm really annoyed that
i can't go there straight

boredom is not
to be feared but
i haven't opened the book
i brought with me
not a single page
seasonal wind   umbrella broke
i dropped   my gloves
found them   right away

this isn't my room
it clears for just a moment
the birds scatter and dance
all the alleys are familiar
you musn't love
the harbors you pass through
i don't want to know a place
for just one night
i find changelessness beautiful
they say all the world's
lost children stop by here
together, everyone,
delightedly gets lost

Train #2214

in this way gradually
becoming only the goal
in order to do what i am to do
i sway with the movement of
a different train

the tall girl
wearing a red hood
fell asleep
my neighbor for just two hours
her voice when talking
on the phone
truly enchanting
laughing "Si, si, si, si!"
in a thin, raspy voice
like breathing
as if about to expire
facing backward
the mountain range is enshrined
in the left hand window
perhaps the Alps
they are too extravagant
so i pretend i didn't see them
the Adriatic Sea fills
the window on the right

i continue to move
from town to town
from town to island
in this way gradually
becoming only the goal
in order to do what i am to do
when a landscape dies
i display it in a black picture frame

i may be terribly tired
soon to arrive at
Santa Lucia station

Jumbled forest

the rain continues
but it is supposed to clear from noon
this is a small island but
we hurry and when we come out
on the avenue
the blue sky is peeled back
and amidst the clamor
we buy bread and water
there is no gap whatsoever for lunch

each time the body rejoices
there is another stripping away
why did we end up coming
to such a place as this?

this small, inside-out island
is wounded
and calm
and will someday disappear

those children
have been waiting so long
a stout old woman
points and yells
her voice quite loud
and grating
she has certainly
sat long enough
to almost become part
of the wooden chair
in the post office
joy prompting
the stripping away

where in the world
could i be?

swaying with the movement
of the water taxi
we verge on saturation

To the island of graves

when you get off the boat
an island of aligned churches and graves
the whispering of birds and
pristine light
names are solemnly carved
and ordered
there is nothing more beautiful
anywhere
a lifeless island of graves

the next morning
i wake to the voices of gulls
they are clamorous gulls
now and then another voice mixes in
i think i am being called

the next morning
i buy white and yellow flowers
and head for the island of graves
because i will never know anything
more beautiful than this
i commit an evil deed

Hotel Elite

as if in ritual
i search for a postbox
while it's still dark
crawl out of bed
write letters
the temperature and humidity
two letters per day

the tower tilts
it is most lovely at dusk
they tell me
the rain never stops
i almost slip on the stone pavement
you extend a hand

not in the left but the right
side of the postbox
the address left uncertain
it would be fine with me
if it just got lost

on the gentle street
our great change was such
that we didn't mind getting
a little wet

something i had forgotten

I am culpable

waiting for the plane
from Amsterdam
six more hours to go
as i am about to leave
the clear sky arrives
you must not kill the moon bear
i am warned
in a language i don't know
you must not kill the moon bear

even as i whine that
there isn't enough time
unexpectedly granted six hours
i fall silent
you must not kill the moon bear
it is certainly not good to kill one
in which case
what would it be alright to kill?

in this small airport
the people who head off
and the people who arrive
maintain the same speed
clouds have gathered

the expiring brilliance
is frightening
i kept on and
feigning blindness
killed a moon bear

Thick fog

from Bologna to Forli
night comes and i
close the shutters tight
even when morning comes
this still dark room

the indistinct brightness
of trees and vineyards
overflowing with fog
i finally know
that morning has arrived
only after opening the shutters
the finest silence

i have a fever
the ceiling is close
the neighbors give no
sign of life
so i guess they're still sleeping
the town, the birds, time itself
hide any sign of life

i want to open
all the shutters right now
i want to yell:
morning has come!

Spring storm

you who were just born yesterday
are born again today

surrounded by white walls
with a severe expression
delightedly
without my involvement
you are born
every day

gathering the gazes of the many
without me involving myself
you will again be born
tomorrow
remaining uninvolved
lit by the light of the western sun
i walked on the cold wound
of the winter sky
i go to buy sugar candies
in celebration
choosing the sweetest ones

when i return
you are curled up
in a circle
enveloped in the soft light
of the western sun
waiting in order
to be born again
delightedly
with a severe expression
without my involvement

Straße des 17. Juni

Todd is an American
but his Japanese is very good
i am a poet so i think
my Japanese must be odd

we walk with our backs to the wall
we walk along the square
lined with cold graveyards
our backs to Straße des 17. Juni

Todd is an American
but his Japanese is very good
which makes me feel strange
and more, he has a detailed
sense of direction
i am a poet so i don't
worry about directions
(and often fail to find my way)

in this city scarred by war
we talk about
the wars now going on
with a good meal before us
we talk about war

Todd is an American
but his Japanese is very good
and more, his face
has fine features
we continue to talk about war
we are not countries, but people
we continue talking about war

To the north

as soon as i arrive
i squat down, collapsing,
holding my stomach
this might be labor

take me to that harbor town
you just have to take me there
that's all
i'm not asking you
to become a father so
please take me there

with this earnest request
i collapsed
when i came to
no one was there
my body had dried out

this might be labor
i'm not asking you
to become a father
because this is the outcome
i sought for myself

please just come up
with a new name

ATTENZION
QUESTO TAXI

Ibis Hotel

three days passed away
and with them
a high fever
three days
the equivalent
of a mere sigh

the women who
line up at the show windows
revealing in bathing suits call out:
is there something, you want, to ask me?
when the questions overflow
it is as if there were none
on to the next window

when i come out
onto the avenue having bought
not a woman
but bread, yogurt and herring,
the same dog
invariably follows me
a dog with short white fur
even if i come out
onto the avenue having bought
a postcard
the same dog
invariably follows me:
is there something, you want, to ask me?

i have all kinds of questions but
when the questions overflow
it is as if there were none
if asked, lover or stranger?
since the answer is stranger
i keep the question to myself
glancing over
at the tail of the same dog
on to the next window

on to the next town

Train #2348

emerging from a blue cave
to the central station
from central station to central station
we pass through forests
of thin silhouettes
it is a landscape in which
a precipitate of tranquil blue
has settled

riding the veins
deciding our roles
you are a platelet
so protect against
any and all wounds
a red blood cell
i advance without cease

it is a landscape
pregnant with blue
like a forest started from
amputated horse legs
lined up and fossilized

riding the veins
advancing without end
even while losing
outline and form
emerging from a blue cave
we may be foolish
but we are still worth living

Sundial

tilting at an acute angle
reflecting
not absorbing
receiving as is
flowing along the
stone pavement
the light is
not a guide

they should disappear
they should all disappear
everything is enemy
you must not
let down your guard
at the beautiful outer wall
when this body
becomes a second hand
then, for the first time,
things will go well

not a guide
flowing with whittled-down thought
the light goes away
as if fleeing
it is fleeing
intoning they should all disappear
i firmly bind
my tear ducts
whose fault is this?

Blackbirds

whistling
you let me know
there are many birds' nests
around here
but half of them
are unoccupied

the place to which
you and i
return just once
no room for whistling
still tense
carrying a branch
turning away to ignore
we sleep in this place
holding hands

South of the Spree River

holding my knees
i am watching the
washing machine go around
it gets dark late
so you mustn't misunderstand

when they touch stillness
people fall silent
not empty
randomly overflowing
if we choose freedom
we cannot choose
anything but freedom
there was nothing
that needed to be done

and then
the washing machine
picks up speed
still holding my knees
peacefully abiding
i become a fossil
still watching the
washing machine
peacefully abiding
i become a fossil

Alexanderplatz Station

not knowing for several days
that someone had died
there was no surprise
in finding out

at a flower shop
near the World Clock
i buy flowers
and arrange them
they fall apart and scatter
"antique market" written
in a clumsy hand
stopping in
the proprietor is kind

swaying with
the salt, soups, books
of daily life
in hand
a young boy is crying
clutching his ankles
not knowing for several days
that someone had died
there was no surprise
in finding out
i get ready
am easily angered

am i unfeeling?

Anywhere to be found

the two of us going
to someplace far away
to a place no longer there
where boundless feelings
lie buried
to someplace far away

overflowing with birds
there is no voice
nor any shouts
a place no longer there

eating sweets
we walk back
sweets alone are not enough
we look for a place
to have dinner

no need to
wrack your brain
trying to learn
but there are
anywhere to be found
the warm ones and
ones that don't even
cast a shadow are
anywhere to be found

perhaps now

The room of 18 April

i wasn't good
with birthdays
they tend to slip my mind
so i said
i'm not good with them
now, however,
that might not be the case

i wrap myself in cloth
to avoid the sun
not negation
i only affirm
wrapping myself in cloth
i'm just living

while there are limits
to what can be called spring
i might be permitted
to laugh
i affirm

Moving away from the linden tree

as things gets serious
i let them go
because i can't avert my gaze
i close my eyes

under the eaves
of a coffee shop
we talked on
about nothing in particular
concerned about the time
but there was no clock

before it gets dark
we climb the tower
and take in the last town
after taking it in for a while
i close my eyes
it isn't that the days disappear
it is i who leave

before filling to overflowing
i stick in
a sewing needle

Water landing

when you deliberately cry
even though you
don't want to cry
you sell your soul
you're too fast
so you forget right away

from forest to town
to sea   to sky
the one choosing
these shifting names
is me

the one choosing
to live or to die
is me
above the clouds
the unvarying temperature
humidity
the sunset forms a circle
and rebounds

i deliberately cried
even though i
didn't want to cry
i remember it
being too quick

the sold soul
throws itself
into the night
that is most beautiful
having sunk
silently going
back and forth
feigning calm
immediately after
i repeatedly choose
even though
i don't want to cry,
cry

Something I've recently realized is how well I've come to get along with myself. I have continued writing poems, and nine years have passed since my first collection was published. There are many people who love my first collection of poems, and this is something that makes me very happy. People often want me to write something with the same feeling as those poems, but I have come to get along quite well with myself. To the point that I can even look back on those poems with a particular affection.

I think things move with great speed. My surroundings and my mind undergo great change and, since I've stopped resisting this, the speed only increases daily. In this way, moving past my feelings of having become something of a hermit, wanting to be like a just-born infant, I thought I would travel and write poems daily. It even seemed that unless I did this, I would not be able to move forward. I was, after all, not a hermit, but a 30-year-old poet, turning 31 during my travels.

In the process of coming to get along well with myself, there was inevitably the presence of neighbors. Living in cheap, wood-framed apartments, there were neighbors on the other side of a single, thin wall, and we passed our unrelated days. At night, we lived mutually considerate of each other's lives. That, if you think about it, is a truly peculiar kind of presence. I continued to find solace in that peculiar presence. That peculiar relation of an unrelated someone living next-door.

While traveling, neighbors change every day and are just people in transit. It is as if no one were there, and that is part of the theme of this collection of poems. I am facing myself more.

I am truly indebted to Kameoka-san who, for the past nine years, has watched over the process by which I have come to get along with myself. I am once again deeply grateful.

I thank all those who were involved in this collection: My thoroughly inobtrusive companion, those who made the travel arrangements, the family members who pretended not to notice my self-centeredness. If you see me about to start a fight with myself, please intervene. Because I will come back. I have turned nine years old.

AFTERWORD

Water take-off *2013.3.24 Ljubljana, Slovenia*
The path to Tivoli Park *2013.3.25 Ljubljana, Slovenia*
Shallow sleep *2013.3.26 Ljubljana, Slovenia*
Standing on the surface of the lake *2013.3.27 Ljubljana, Slovenia*
The path to Tivoli Park 2 *2013.3.28 Ljubljana, Slovenia*
A quality cuisine *2013.3.29 Ljubljana, Slovenia*
Sabbath *2013.3.30 Ljubljana, Slovenia*
The time of bones *2013.3.31 Ljubljana, Slovenia*
At port *2013.4.1 Trieste, Italia*
Train #2214 *2013.4.2 Venezia, Italia*
Jumbled forest *2013.4.3 Venezia, Italia*
To the island of graves *2013.4.4 Bologna, Italia*
Hotel Elite *2013.4.5 Bologna, Italia*
I am culpable *2013.4.6 Forlì, Italia*
Thick fog *2013.4.7 Forlì, Italia*
Spring storm *2013.4.8 Berlin, Deutschland*
Straße des 17. Juni *2013.4.9 Berlin, Deutschland*
To the north *2013.4.10 Hamburg, Deutschland*
Ibis Hotel *2013.4.11 Hamburg, Deutschland*
Train #2348 *2013.4.12 Bielefeld, Deutschland*
Sundial *2013.4.13 Bielefeld, Deutschland*
Blackbirds *2013.4.14 Berlin, Deutschland*
South of the Spree River *2013.4.15 Berlin, Deutschland*
Alexanderplatz Station *2013.4.16 Berlin, Deutschland*
Anywhere to be found *2013.4.17 Berlin, Deutschland*
The room of 18 April *2013.4.18 Berlin, Deutschland*

DATA

I get lost in these poems. That is one of their pleasures. Misumi Mizuki's language is at once plain and unusual. It is plain on the surface and unusual as you enter it. Like all good poetry, these poems offer the choice of staying behind or being taken along. In either case, the invitation stands. Misumi makes full use of the character of Japanese grammar which can leave the subject as well as start and finish of sentences open. These are some of the qualities I have sought to bring into the English renderings. I think they are integral to a poet and poems at once intensely private but, when it comes to it, not afraid of being seen.

TRANSLATOR'S NOTE